CW00746556

AN ANTHOLOGY OF
Love Poems

ILLUSTRATED WITH PHOTOGRAPHS FROM
THE FRANCIS FRITH COLLECTION

Chosen and edited by
Terence and Eliza Sackett

First published in the United Kingdom in 2003 by
Black Horse Books (an imprint of the Frith Book Company)

This revised and updated edition published by the
Frith Book Company in 2005

Text and Design copyright © Frith Book Company Ltd
Photographs copyright © The Francis Frith Collection

The Frith photographs and the Frith logo are reproduced under licence
from Heritage Photographic Resources Ltd, the owners of the
Frith archive and trademarks.

All rights reserved. No photograph in this publication may be sold to a third
party other than in the original form of this publication, or framed for sale to a
third party. No parts of this publication may be reproduced, stored in a retrieval
system, or transmitted, in any form, or by any means, electronic, mechanical,
photocopying, recording or otherwise, without the prior
permission of the publishers and copyright holder.

British Library Cataloguing in Publication Data
An Anthology of Love Poems
Chosen and edited by Terence and Eliza Sackett
1-84589-002-7

Although the publishers have tried to contact all copyright holders before
publication, this has not proved possible in every case. If notified, the
publisher will be pleased to make any necessary arrangements.

Frith Book Company
Frith's Barn, Teffont,
Salisbury, Wiltshire SP3 5QP
Tel: +44 (0) 1722 716 376
Email: info@francisfrith.co.uk
www.francisfrith.co.uk

Dorchester, Hangmans Cottage 1913 65618p

The colour-tinting is for illustrative purposes only, and is not intended to be historically accurate

Printed and bound in England

Contents

The First Day

I WISH I could remember the first day,
First hour, first moment of your meeting me,
If bright or dim the season, it might be
Summer or Winter for aught I can say;
So unrecorded did it slip away,
So blind was I to see and to foresee,
So dull to mark the budding of my tree
That would not blossom yet for many a May,
If only I could recollect it, such
A day of days! I let it come and go
As traceless as a thaw of bygone snow;
It seemed to mean so little, meant so much;
If only now I could recall that touch,
First touch of hand in hand.—Did one but know!

CHRISTINA ROSSETTI (1830-1894)

The Je Ne Sais Quoi

YES, I'm in love, I feel it now,
And Celia has undone me;
And yet I'll swear I can't tell how,
The pleasing plague stole on me.

'Tis not her face that love creates,
For there no Graces revel;
'Tis not her shape, for there the Fates
Have rather been uncivil.

'Tis not her air, for sure in that,
There's nothing more than common;
And all her sense is only chat,
Like any other woman.

Her voice, her touch, might give the alarm—
'Tis both perhaps, or neither;
In short, 'tis that provoking charm
Of Celia altogether.

WILLIAM WHITEHEAD (1715-1785)

The Enchantment

I DID but look and love awhile,
'Twas but for one half-hour:
Then to resist I had no will,
And now I have no power.

To sigh and wish is all my ease;
Sighs which do heat impart
Enough to melt the coldest ice,
Yet cannot warm your heart.

O would your pity give my heart
One corner of your breast,
'Twould learn of yours the winning art,
And quickly steal the rest.

THOMAS OTWAY (1652-1685)

II

I'll O'ertake Thee

ART thou gone in haste?
I'll not forsake thee!
Runnest thou ne'er so fast,
I'll o'ertake thee!
O'er the dales or the downs,
Through the green meadows,
From the fields, through the towns,
To the dim shadows!

All along the plain,
To the low fountains;
Up and down again,
From the high mountains:
Echo, then, shall again
Tell her I follow,
And the floods to the woods
Carry my holla.
Holla!
Ce! la! ho! ho! hu!

JOHN WEBSTER (1580?-1638)
WILLIAM ROWLEY (1585?-1642?)
from The Thracian Wonder

The Sun Rising

BUSY old fool, unruly Sun,
Why dost thou thus,
Through windows, and through curtains, call on us?
Must to thy motions lovers' seasons run?
Saucy pedantic wretch, go chide
Late school-boys and sour prentices,
Go tell court-huntsmen that the king will ride,
Call country ants to harvest offices;
Love, all alike, no season knows nor clime,
Nor hours, days, months, which are the rags of time.

Thy beams so reverend and strong
Why shouldst thou think?
I could eclipse and cloud them with a wink,
But that I would not lose her sight so long.
If her eyes have not blinded thine,
Look, and to-morrow late, tell me,
Whether both th' Indias of spice and mine
Be where thou leftst them, or lie here with me.
Ask for those kings whom thou saw'st yesterday,
And thou shalt hear, 'All here in one bed lay.'

She's all states, and all princes I;
Nothing else is;
Princes do but play us; compared to this,

All honour's mimic, all wealth alchemy.
Thou, Sun, art half as happy as we,
In that the world's contracted thus;
Thine age asks ease, and since thy duties be
To warm the world, that's done in warming us.
Shine here to us, and thou art everywhere;
This bed thy centre is, these walls thy sphere.

JOHN DONNE (1572-1631)

The Good-Morrow

I WONDER by my troth, what thou, and I
Did, till we lov'd? were we not wean'd till then?
But suck'd on country pleasures, childishly?
Or snorted we in the seven sleepers' den?
'Twas so; but this, all pleasures fancies be.
If ever any beauty I did see,
Which I desir'd, and got, 'twas but a dream of thee.

And now good morrow to our waking souls,
Which watch not one another out of fear;
For love, all love of other sights controls,
And makes one little room, an everywhere.
Let sea-discoverers to new worlds have gone;
Let maps to other, worlds on worlds have shown,
Let us possess one world, each hath one, and is one.

My face in thine eye, thine in mine appears,
And true plain hearts do in the faces rest;
Where can we find two better hemispheres
Without sharp north, without declining west?
Whatever dies, was not mix'd equally;
If our two loves be one, or, thou and I
Love so alike, that none do slacken, none can die.

JOHN DONNE (1572-1631)

Go, Lovely Rose

GO, lovely rose—
Tell her that wastes her time and me,
That now she knows,
When I resemble her to thee,
How sweet and fair she seems to be.

Tell her that's young,
And shuns to have her graces spied,
That hadst thou sprung
In deserts where no men abide,
Thou must have uncommended died.

Small is the worth
Of beauty from the light retired:
Bid her come forth,
Suffer her self to be desired,
And not blush so to be admired.

Then die!—that she
The common fate of all things rare
May read in thee;
How small a part of time they share
That are so wondrous sweet and fair!

EDMUND WALLER (1606-1687)

Cherry-Ripe

THERE is a garden in her face
Where roses and white lilies grow;
A heavenly paradise is that place,
Wherein all pleasant fruits do flow;
There cherries grow which none may buy,
Till 'Cherry-ripe' themselves do cry.

Those cherries fairly do enclose
Of orient pearls a double row,
Which when her lovely laughter shows,
They look like rose-buds fill'd with snow:
Yet them nor peer nor prince can buy,
Till 'Cherry-ripe' themselves do cry.

Her eyes like angels watch them still;
Her brows like bended bows do stand,
Threat'ning with piercing frowns to kill
All that attempt with eye or hand
Those sacred cherries to come nigh,
—Till 'Cherry-ripe' themselves do cry!

THOMAS CAMPION (1567-1620)

Cakes and Ale

I GAVE her cakes; I gave her ale,
I gave her sack and sherry;
I kissed her once, I kissed her twice,
And we were wondrous merry.

I gave her beads and bracelets fine,
And I gave her gold down derry;
I thought she was afeard till she stroked my beard,
And we were wondrous merry.

Merry my heart, my cocks, my sprights,
Merry my hey down derry;
I kissed her once and I kissed her twice,
And we were wondrous merry.

ANON

Then I Was in Love

ONCE did my thoughts both ebb and flow,
As passion did them move;
Once did I hope, straight fear again,—
And then I was in love.

Once did I waking spend the night,
And tell how many minutes move;
Once did I wishing waste the day,—
And then I was in love …

Once did I breathe another's breath
And in my mistress move;
Once was I not mine own at all,—
And then I was in love …

ANON

What 'Tis to Love

PHEBE. Good shepherd, tell this youth what 'tis to love.
Silvius. It is to be made of sighs and tears;
And so am I for Phebe.
Phebe. And I for Ganymede.
Orlando. And I for Rosalind.
Rosalind. And I for no woman.
Silvius. It is to be all made of faith and service;
And so am I for Phebe.
Phebe. And I for Ganymede.
Orlando. And I for Rosalind.
Rosalind. And I for no woman.
Silvius. It is to be all made of fantasy,
All made of passion, and all made of wishes;
All adoration, duty, and observance,
All humbleness, all patience, and impatience,
All purity, all trial, all observance;
And so am I for Phebe.

WILLIAM SHAKESPEARE (1564-1616)
from As You Like It

Speak, Gentle Heart

SPEAK, gentle heart, where is thy dwelling place?
With her, whose birth the heavens themselves have blest.
What dost thou there? Sometimes behold her face,
And lodge sometimes within her crystal breast:
She cold, thou hot, how can you then agree?
Not nature now, but love doth govern me.

With her wilt thou remain, and let me die?
If I return, we both shall die for grief:
If still thou stay, what good shall grow thereby?
I'll move her heart to purchase thy relief:
What if her heart be hard, and stop his ears?
I'll sigh aloud, and make him soft with tears:

If that prevail, wilt thou return from thence?
Not I alone, her heart shall come with me:
Then will you both live under my defence?
So long as life will let us both agree:
Why then despair?—go pack thee hence away,
I live in hope to have a golden day.

THOMAS WATSON (1557?-1592)

The Flame Within

I FEED a flame within, which so torments me,
That it both pains my heart, and yet contents me:
'Tis such a pleasing smart, and I so love it,
That I had rather die than once remove it.

Yet he for whom I grieve shall never know it;
My heart does not betray, nor my eyes show it.
Not a sigh, nor a tear, my pain discloses,
But they fall silently, like dew on roses.

Thus, to prevent my love from being cruel,
My heart's the sacrifice, as 'tis the fuel:
And while I suffer thus to give him quiet,
My faith rewards my love, though he deny it.

On his eyes will I gaze, and there delight me;
While I conceal my love no frown can fright me.
To be more happy I dare not aspire,
Nor can I fall more low, mounting no higher.

JOHN DRYDEN (1631-1700)
from Secret Love

Oh, What is Longer than the Way?

OH, what is longer than the way?
And what is deeper than the sea?
And what is louder than the horn?
And what is sharper than the thorn?
And what is greener than the grass?
And what is worse than a woman was?

Oh, Love is longer than the way,
And hell is deeper than the sea,
And thunder is louder than the horn,
And hunger is sharper than the thorn,
And poison is greener than the grass,
And the devil is worse than a woman was.

ANON

Love Lives in the Moony Light

I THOUGHT Love lived in the hot sunshine,
But O, he lives in the moony light!
I thought to find Love in the heat of day,
But sweet Love is the comforter of night.

Seek Love in the pity of other's woe,
In the gentle relief of another's care,
In the darkness of night and the winter's snow,
With the nakcd and outcast   seek Love there.

WILLIAM BLAKE (1757-1827)
from William Bond

Absence

WHEN my love was away,
Full three days were not sped,
I caught my fancy astray
Thinking if she were dead,

And I alone, alone:
It seemed in my misery
In all the world was none
Ever so lone as I.

I wept; but it did not shame
Nor comfort my heart: away
I rode as I might, and came
To my love at close of day.

The sight of her stilled my fears,
My fairest-hearted love:
And yet in her eyes were tears:
Which when I questioned of,

O now thou art come, she cried,
'Tis fled: but I thought to-day
I never could here abide,
If thou wert longer away.

ROBERT BRIDGES (1844-1930)

Come Back to Me in Dreams

COME to me in the silence of the night;
Come in the speaking silence of a dream;
Come with soft rounded cheeks and eyes as bright
As sunlight on a stream;
Come back in tears,
O memory, hope, love of finished years.

O dream how sweet, too sweet, too bitter sweet,
Whose wakening should have been in Paradise,
Where souls brimfull of love abide and meet;
Where thirsting longing eyes
Watch the slow door
That opening, letting in, lets out no more.

Yet come to me in dreams, that I may live
My very life again though cold in death:
Come back to me in dreams, that I may give
Pulse for pulse, breath for breath:
Speak low, lean low,
As long ago, my love, how long ago.

CHRISTINA ROSSETTI (1830-1894)

In an Artist's Studio

ONE face looks out from all his canvasses,
One selfsame figure sits or walks or leans:
We found her hidden just behind those screens,
That mirror gave back all her loveliness.
A queen in opal or in ruby dress,
A nameless girl in freshest summer-greens,
A saint, an angel—every canvas means
The same one meaning, neither more nor less.
He feeds upon her face by day and night,
And she with true kind eyes looks back on him,
Fair as the moon and joyful as the light:
Not wan with waiting, not with sorrow dim;
Not as she is, but was when hope shone bright;
Not as she is, but as she fills his dream.

CHRISTINA ROSSETTI (1830-1894)

The Lover in Winter Plaineth
for the Spring

O WESTERN wind, when wilt thou blow,
That the small rain down can rain?
Christ, that my love were in my arms
And I in my bed again!

ANON

Robin Adair

WHAT'S this dull town to me?
Robin's not near;
What was't I wished to see,
What wished to hear?
Where's all the joy and mirth
That made this town heaven on earth?
Oh! they're all fled with thee,
Robin Adair.

What made the assembly shine?
Robin Adair;
What made the ball so fine?
Robin was there.
What, when the play was o'er,
What made my heart so sore?
Oh! it was parting with
Robin Adair.

But now thou art far from me,
Robin Adair;
And now I never see
Robin Adair;
Yet he I love so well,
Still in my heart shall dwell,
Oh! I can ne'er forget
Robin Adair.

LADY CAROLINE KEPPEL (1735-?)

Summer Dawn

PRAY but one prayer for me 'twixt thy closed lips,
Think but one thought of me up in the stars.
The summer night waneth, the morning light slips,
Faint and gray 'twixt the leaves of the aspen,
betwixt the cloud-bars,
That are patiently waiting there for the dawn:
Patient and colourless, though Heaven's gold
Waits to float through them along with the sun.
Far out in the meadows, above the young corn,
The heavy elms wait, and restless and cold
The uneasy wind rises; the roses are dun;
Through the long twilight they pray for the dawn,
Round the lone house in the midst of the corn.
Speak but one word to me over the corn,
Over the tender, bowed locks of the corn.

WILLIAM MORRIS (1834-1896)

The Rose of Sharon

I AM the rose of Sharon,
and the lily of the valleys.
As the lily among thorns,
so is my love among the daughters.
As the apple tree among the trees of the wood,
so is my beloved among the sons.
I sat down under his shadow with great delight,
and his fruit was sweet to my taste.
He brought me to the banqueting house,
and his banner over me was love.
Stay me with flagons, comfort me with apples:
for I am sick of love.
His left hand is under my head,
and his right hand doth embrace me.

from The Song of Songs

My Beloved Spake

MY BELOVED spake, and said unto me,
Rise up, my love, my fair one, and come away.
For, lo, the winter is past,
the rain is over and gone;
The flowers appear on the earth;
the time of the singing of birds is come,
and the voice of the turtle is heard in our land;
The fig tree putteth forth her green figs,
and the vines with the tender grape give a good smell.
Arise, my love, my fair one, and come away …
My beloved is mine, and I am his:
he feedeth among the lilies.
Until the day break, and the shadows flee away,
turn, my beloved, and be thou like a roe or a young hart upon
the mountains of Bether.

from The Song of Songs

Silent Noon

YOUR hands lie open in the long fresh grass,—
The finger-points look through like rosy blooms:
Your eyes smile peace. The pasture gleams and glooms
'Neath billowing skies that scatter and amass.
All round our nest, far as the eye can pass,
Are golden kingcup-fields with silver edge
Where the cow-parsley skirts the hawthorn-hedge.
'Tis visible silence, still as the hour-glass.

Deep in the sun-searched growths the dragon-fly
Hangs like a blue thread loosened from the sky:—
So this winged hour is dropped to us from above.
Oh! clasp we to our hearts, for deathless dower,
This close-companioned inarticulate hour
When twofold silence was the song of love.

DANTE GABRIEL ROSSETTI (1828-1882)
from The House of Life

The Ecstacy

Where, like a pillow on a bed,
A pregnant bank swelled up, to rest
The violet's reclining head,
Sat we two, one another's best.
Our hands were firmly cemented
With a fast balm, which thence did spring,
Our eye-beams twisted, and did thread
Our eyes, upon one double string;
So to engraft our hands, as yet
Was all the means to make us one;
And pictures in our eyes to get
Was all our propagation.
As, 'twixt two equal armies, Fate
Suspends uncertain victory,
Our souls—which to advance their state,
Were gone out—hung 'twixt her and me.
And whilst our souls negotiate there,
We like sepulchral statues lay;
All day, the same our postures were,
And we said nothing, all the day …

JOHN DONNE (1572-1631)

Wholly Thine

DOST ask (my dear) what service I will have?
To love me day and night is all I crave,
To dream on me, to expect, to think on me,
Depend and hope, still covet me to see,
Delight thyself in me, be wholly mine,
For know, my love, that I am wholly thine.

TERENCE (BC190-159)
TRANSLATED BY ROBERT BURTON (1577-1640)
from the Anatomy of Melancholy

A Divine Rapture

E'EN like two little bank-dividing brooks,
That wash the pebbles with their wanton streams,
And having ranged and searched a thousand nooks,
Meet both at length in silver-breasted Thames,
Where in a greater current they conjoin:
So I my Best-Beloved's am; so he is mine.

E'en so we met; and after long pursuit,
E'en so we joined; we both became entire;
No need for either to renew a suit,
For I was flax, and he was flames of fire:
Our firm-united souls did more than twine;
So I my Best-Beloved's am; so he is mine.

If all those glittering monarchs that command
The servile quarters of this earthly ball,
Should tender in exchange, their shares of land,
I would not change my fortunes for them all:
Their wealth is but a counter to my coin:
The world's but theirs; but my Beloved's mine.

FRANCIS QUARLES (1592-1644)

A Beauty Spot

FAUSTINA hath a spot on her face,
Mixed with sweet beauty, making for her grace.
By what sweet influence it was begot,
I know not; but it is a spotless spot.

THOMAS BASTARD

From Sally in our Alley

OF ALL the girls that are so smart
There's none like pretty Sally;
She is the darling of my heart,
And she lives in our alley.
There is no lady in the land
Is half so sweet as Sally;
She is the darling of my heart,
And she lives in our alley ...

Of all the days that's in the week
I dearly love but one day—
And that's the day that comes betwixt
A Saturday and Monday:
For then I'm dressed all in my best
To walk abroad with Sally;
She is the darling of my heart,
And she lives in our alley ...

When Christmas comes about again,
O then I shall have money!
I'll hoard it up, and box and all
I'll give it to my honey:
I would it were ten thousand pounds;
I'd give it all to Sally;
She is the darling of my heart,
And she lives in our alley ...

HENRY CAREY (1687-1743)

To Helen

HELEN, thy beauty is to me
Like those Nicean barks of yore
That gently, o'er a perfumed sea,
The weary way-worn wanderer bore
To his own native shore.

On desperate seas long wont to roam,
Thy hyacinth hair, thy classic face,
Thy Naiad airs have brought me home
To the glory that was Greece,
And the grandeur that was Rome.

Lo, in yon brilliant window-niche
How statue-like I see thee stand,
The agate lamp within thy hand!
Ah! Psyche, from the regions which
Are holy land!

EDGAR ALLEN POE (1809-1849)

That Ever I Saw

MY LADY is a pretty one,
A pretty pretty pretty one;
My lady is a pretty one
As ever I saw.

She is gentle and also wise;
Of all other she beareth the prize,
That ever I saw.

To hear her sing, to see her dance!
She will the best herself advance,
That ever I saw.

To see her fingers that be so small!
In my conceit she passeth all
That ever I saw.

Nature in her hath wonderly wrought.
Christ never such another bought,
That ever I saw.

I have seen many that have beauty,
Yet is there none like to my lady
That ever I saw.

Therefore I dare this boldly say,
I shall have the best and fairest may
That ever I saw.

ANON

I Falsehood Loved

THE GARDENER standing by,
Proffered to choose for me
The pink, the primrose, and the rose,
But I refused the three.
The primrose I forsook
Because it came too soon,
The violet I overlooked
And vowed to wait till June.

In June the red rose sprung,
But was no flower for me;
I plucked it up, lo! by the stalk,
And planted the willow tree.
The willow I now must wear,
With sorrows twined among,
That all the world may know
I falsehood loved too long.

ANON

Why am I always The Bridesmaid?

WHY AM I dressed in these beautiful clothes?
What is the matter with me?
I've been the bridesmaid for twenty-two brides;
This time'll make twenty-three.
Twenty-two ladies I've helped off the shelf;
No doubt it seems a bit strange:
Being the bridesmaid is no good to me;
And I think I could do with a change.

Why am I always the bridesmaid?
Never the blushing bride?
Ding-dong! wedding bells
Only ring for other gels;
But some fine day—
Oh, let it be soon!—
I shall wake up in the morning
On my own honeymoon.

CHARLES COLLINS AND FRED W LEIGH 1917

On Monsieur's Departure

I GRIEVE, and dare not show my discontent;
I love, and yet am forced to seem to hate;
I do, yet dare not say I ever meant;
I seem stark mute, but inwardly do prate:
I am, and not; I freeze, and yet am burned,
Since from myself, my other self I turned.

My care is like my shadow in the sun,
Follows me flying, flies when I pursue it;
Stands and lies by me, does what I have done;
This too familiar care does make me rue it:
No means I find to rid him from my breast,
Till by the end of things it be suppressed.

Some gentler passions slide into my mind,
For I am soft, and made of melting snow;
Oh be more cruel, Love, and so be kind;
Let me or float or sink, be high or low:
Or let me live with some more sweet content,
Or die, and so forget what love e'er meant.

QUEEN ELIZABETH I (1558-1603)

A Young Wife

THE PAIN of loving you
Is almost more than I can bear.
I walk in fear of you.
The darkness starts up where
You stand, and the night comes through
Your eyes when you look at me.
Ah never before did I see
The shadows that live in the sun!
Now every tall glad tree
Turns round its back to the sun
And looks down on the ground, to see
The shadow it used to shun.
At the foot of each glowing thing
A night lies looking up.
Oh, and I want to sing
And dance, but I can't lift up
My eyes from the shadows: dark
They lie spilt round the cup.

What is it?—Hark
The faint fine seethe in the air!
Like the seething sound in a shell!
It is death still seething where
The wild-flower shakes its bell
And the skylark twinkles blue—
The pain of loving you
Is almost more than I can bear.

D H LAWRENCE (1885-1930)

On the Departure Platform

WE KISSED at the barrier; and passing through
She left me, and moment by moment got
Smaller and smaller, until to my view
She was but a spot;

A wee white spot of muslin fluff
That down the diminishing platform bore
Through hustling crowds of gentle and rough
To the carriage door.

Under the lamplight's fitful glowers,
Behind dark groups from far and near,
Whose interests were apart from ours,
She would disappear,

Then show again, till I ceased to see
That flexible form, that nebulous white;
And she who was more than my life to me
Had vanished quite.

We have penned new plans since that fair fond day,
And in season she will appear again—
Perhaps in the same soft white array—
But never as then!

—'And why, young man, must eternally fly
A joy you'll repeat, if you love her well?'
—O friend, nought happens twice thus: why,
I cannot tell!

THOMAS HARDY (1840-1928)

Budmouth Dears

WHEN we lay where Budmouth Beach is,
O, the girls were fresh as peaches,
With their tall and tossing figures and their eyes of blue and brown!
And our hearts would ache with longing
As we paced from our sing-songing,
With a smart Clink! Clink! up the Esplanade and down.

They distracted and delayed us
By the pleasant pranks they played us,
And what marvel, then, if troopers, even of regiments of renown,
On whom flashed those eyes divine, O,
Should forget the countersign, O,
As we tore Clink! Clink! back to camp above the town?

Do they miss us much, I wonder,
Now that war has swept us sunder,
And we roam from where the faces smile to where the faces frown?
And no more behold the features
Of the fair fantastic creatures,
And no more Clink! Clink! past the parlours of the town?

Shall we once again there meet them?
Falter fond attempts to greet them?
Will the gay sling-jacket glow again beside the muslin gown?
Will they archly quiz and con us
With a sideway glance upon us,
While our spurs Clink! Clink! up the Esplanade and down?

THOMAS HARDY (1840-1928)

Jeanie Morrison

I'VE WANDERED east, I've wandered west,
Through mony a weary way;
But never, never can forget
The luve o' life's young day!
The fire that's blawn on Beltane e'en,
May weel be black gin Yule;
But blacker fa' awaits the heart
Where first fond luve grows cule.

O dear, dear Jeanie Morrison,
The thochts o' bygone years
Still fling their shadows owre my path,
And blind my een wi' tears:
They blind my een wi' saut, saut tears,
And sair and sick I pine,
As memory idly summons up
The blythe blinks o' langsyne.

'Twas then we luvit ilk ither weel,
'Twas then we twa did part;
Sweet time—sad time! twa bairns at schule,
Twa bairns, and but ae heart!
'Twas then we sat on ae laigh bink,
To leir ilk ither lear;
And tones, and looks, and smiles were shed,
Remembered evermair.

I wonder, Jeanie, often yet,
When sitting on that bink,
Cheek touchin' cheek, loof locked in loof,
What our wee heads could think!
When baith bent doun owre ae braid page,
Wi' ae buik on our knee,
Thy lips were on thy lesson, but
My lesson was in thee …

My head rins round and round about,
My heart flows like a sea,
As ane by ane the thochts rush back
O' schule-time and o' thee.
O mornin' life! O mornin' luve!
O lichtsome days and lang,
When hinnied hopes around our hearts
Like simmer blossoms sprang! …

WILLIAM MOTHERWELL (1797-1835)

Beltane – May Day; blinks – glimpses, moments;
bink – bench; leir ilk ither lear – hear each other's
lessons; loof – hand

Jenny Kissed Me

JENNY kissed me when we met,
Jumping from the chair she sat in;
Time, you thief, who love to get
Sweets into your list, put that in!
Say I'm weary, say I'm sad,
Say that health and wealth have missed me,
Say I'm growing old, but add,
Jenny kissed me.

J H LEIGH HUNT (1784-1859)

I See You, Juliet, Still

I SEE you, Juliet, still, with your straw hat
Loaded with vines, and with your dear pale face,
On which those thirty years so lightly sat,
And the white outline of your muslin dress.
You wore a little fichu trimmed with lace
And crossed in front, as was the fashion then,
Bound at your waist with a broad band or sash,
All white and fresh and virginally plain.
There was a sound of shouting far away
Down in the valley, as they called to us,
And you, with hands clasped seeming still to pray
Patience of fate, stood listening to me thus
With heaving bosom. There a rose lay curled.
It was the reddest rose in all the world.

WILFRID SCAWEN BLUNT (1840-1922)
from Love Sonnets of Proteus

Take, O Take those Lips Away

TAKE, O take those lips away,
That so sweetly were forsworn,
And those eyes, the break of day,
Lights that do mislead the morn!
But my kisses bring again,
Bring again;
Seals of love, but sealed in vain,
Sealed in vain!

WILLIAM SHAKESPEARE (1564-1616)
from Measure for Measure

Song

A SUNNY shaft did I behold,
From sky to earth it slanted:
And poised therein a bird so bold—
Sweet bird, thou wert enchanted!
He sank, he rose, he twinkled, he trolled
Within that shaft of sunny mist;
His eyes of fire, his beak of gold,
All else of amethyst.

And thus he sang: 'Adieu! adieu!
Love's dreams prove seldom true.
The blossoms, they make no delay:
The sparkling dew-drops will not stay.
Sweet month of May,
We must away;
Far, far away!
To-day! to-day!'

SAMUEL TAYLOR COLERIDGE (1772-1834)

from Ae Fond Kiss

AE FOND kiss, and then we sever;
Ae fareweel, alas, for ever!
Deep in heart-wrung tears I'll pledge thee,
Warring sighs and groans I'll wage thee.

Who shall say that Fortune grieves him,
While the star of hope she leaves him?
Me, nae cheerful twinkle lights me;
Dark despair around benights me …

Fare-thee-weel, thou first and fairest!
Fare-thee-weel, thou best and dearest!
Thine be ilka joy and treasure,
Peace, Enjoyment, Love and Pleasure!

Ae fond kiss, and then we sever!
Ae fareweel alas, for ever!
Deep in heart-wrung tears I'll pledge thee,
Warring sighs and groans I'll wage thee.

ROBERT BURNS (1759-1796)

Sea Love

TIDE be runnin' the great world over:
'Twas only last June month I mind that we
Was thinkin' the toss and the call in the breast of the lover
So everlastin' as the sea.

Heer's the same little fishes that splutter and swim,
Wi' the moon's old glim on the grey, wet sand:
An' him no more to me nor me to him
Than the wind goin' over my hand.

CHARLOTTE MEW (1869-1928)

Does Love Die?

IN OUR old shipwrecked days there was an hour,
When in the firelight steadily aglow,
Joined slackly, we beheld the red chasm grow
Among the clicking coals. Our library-bower
That eve was left to us: and hushed we sat
As lovers to whom Time is whispering.
From sudden-opened doors we heard them sing.
The nodding elders mixed good wine with chat.
Well knew we that Life's greatest treasure lay
With us, and of it was our talk. 'Ah, yes!
Love dies!' I said: I never thought it less.
She yearned to me that sentence to unsay.
Then when the fire domed blackening, I found
Her cheek was salt against my kiss, and swift
Up the sharp scale of sobs her breast did lift:—
Now am I haunted by that taste! that sound!

GEORGE MEREDITH (1828-1909)
from Modern Love

When We Two Parted

When we two parted
In silence and tears,
Half broken-hearted,
To sever for years,
Pale grew thy cheek and cold,
Colder thy kiss;
Truly that hour foretold
Sorrow to this! …

They name thee before me,
A knell to mine ear;
A shudder comes o'er me—
Why wert thou so dear?
They know not I knew thee
Who knew thee too well:
Long, long shall I rue thee
Too deeply to tell.

In secret we met:
In silence I grieve
That thy heart could forget,
Thy spirit deceive.
If I should meet thee
After long years,
How should I greet thee?—
With silence and tears.

LORD BYRON (1788-1824)

I Remember

SOME hang above the tombs,
Some weep in empty rooms,
I, when the iris blooms,
Remember.

I, when the cyclamen
Opens her buds again,
Rejoice a moment—then
Remember.

MARY COLERIDGE (1861-1907)

Whan I Sleep I Dream

WHAN I sleep I dream,
Whan I wauk I'm eerie,
Sleep I canna get,
For thinkin' o' my dearie.

Lanely night comes on,
A' the house are sleeping,
I think on the bonnie lad
That has my heart a keeping.
Ay waukin O, waukin ay and wearie,
Sleep I canna get, for thinkin' o' my dearie.

Lanely night comes on,
A' the house are sleeping,
I think on my bonnie lad,
An' I bleer my een wi' greetin'!
Ay waukin O, waukin ay and wearie,
Sleep I canna get, for thinkin' o' my dearie.

ROBERT BURNS (1759-1796)

Scarborough Fair

WHERE are you going? To Scarborough Fair?
Parsley, sage, rosemary, thyme.
Remember me to a bonny lass there,
For once she was a true lover of mine.

Tell her to make me a cambric shirt,
Parsley, sage, rosemary, thyme.
Without any needle or thread worked in't,
And she shall be a true lover of mine.

Tell her to wash it in yonder well,
Parsley, sage, rosemary, thyme.
Where water ne'er sprung nor a drop of rain fell,
And she shall be a true lover of mine.

Tell her to plough me an acre of land,
Parsley, sage, rosemary, thyme.
Between the sea and the salt sea strand,
And she shall be a true lover of mine.

Tell her to plough it with one ram's horn,
Parsley, sage, rosemary, thyme.
And sow it all over with one peppercorn,
And she shall be a true lover of mine.

Tell her to reap it with a sickle of leather,
Parsley, sage, rosemary, thyme.
And tie it all up with a tom tit's feather,
And she shall be a true lover of mine.

Tell her to gather it all in a sack,
Parsley, sage, rosemary, thyme.
And carry it home on a butterfly's back,
And then she shall be a true lover of mine.

TRADITIONAL

The Ballad-Singer

SING, Ballad-singer, raise a hearty tune;
Make me forget that there was ever a one
I walked with in the meek light of the moon
When the day's work was done.

Rhyme, Ballad-rhymer, start a country song;
Make me forget that she whom I loved well
Swore she would love me dearly, love me long,
Then—what I cannot tell!

Sing, Ballad-singer, from your little book;
Make me forget those heart-breaks, achings, fears;
Make me forget her name, her sweet sweet look—
Make me forget her tears.

THOMAS HARDY (1840-1928)

At Castle Boterel

AS I drive to the junction of lane and highway,
And the drizzle bedrenches the waggonette,
I look behind at the fading byway,
And see on its slope, now glistening wet,
Distinctly yet

Myself and a girlish form benighted
In dry March weather. We climb the road
Beside a chaise. We had just alighted
To ease the sturdy pony's load
When he sighed and slowed.

What we did as we climbed, and what we talked of
Matters not much, nor to what it led,—
Something that life will not be balked of
Without rude reason till hope is dead
And feeling fled.

It filled but a minute. But was there ever
A time of such quality, since or before,
In that hill's story? To one mind never,
Though it has been climbed, foot-swift, foot-sore,
By thousands more.

Primaeval rocks form the road's steep border,
And much have they faced there, first and last,
Of the transitory in Earth's long order;
But what they record in colour and cast
Is—that we two passed.

And to me, though Time's unflinching rigour,
In mindless rote, has ruled from sight
The substance now, one phantom figure
Remains on the slope, as when that night
Saw us alight.

I look and see it there, shrinking, shrinking,
I look back at it amid the rain
For the very last time; for my sand is sinking,
And I shall traverse old love's domain
Never again.

THOMAS HARDY (1840-1928)

Thou Flower of Summer

WHEN in summer thou walkest
In the meads by the river,
And to thyself talkest,
Dost thou think of one ever—
A lost and a lorn one
That adores thee and loves thee?
And when happy morn's gone,
And nature's calm moves thee,
Leaving thee to thy sleep like an angel at rest,
Does the one who adores thee still live in thy breast?

Does nature e'er give thee
Love's past happy vision,
And wrap thee and leave thee
In fancies elysian?
Thy beauty I clung to,
As leaves to the tree;
When thou fair and young too
Looked lightly on me,
Till love came upon thee like the sun to the west
And shed its perfuming and bloom on thy breast.

JOHN CLARE (1793-1864)

I Sought Him Whom My Soul Loveth

BY NIGHT on my bed I sought him whom my soul loveth:
I sought him, but I found him not.
I will rise now, and go about the city in the streets,
and in the broad ways I will seek him whom my soul loveth:
I sought him, but I found him not.
The watchmen that go about the city found me:
to whom I said, Saw ye him whom my soul loveth?
It was but a little that I passed from them,
but I found him whom my soul loveth:
I held him, and would not let him go,
until I had brought him into my mother's house,
and into the chamber of her that conceived me.
I charge you, O ye daughters of Jerusalem,
by the roes, and by the hinds of the field,
that ye stir not up, nor awake my love, till he please.

from The Song of Songs

The Lover Showeth How He is Forsaken

THEY flee from me, that sometime did me seek
With naked foot stalking within my chamber.
Once have I seen them gentle, tame, and meek,
That now are wild, and do not once remember
That sometime they have put themselves in danger,
To take bread at my hand, and now they range,
Busily seeking in continual change.

Thanked be fortune, it hath been otherwise
Twenty times better: but once especial,
In thin array, after a pleasant guise,
When her loose gown did from her shoulders fall,
And she me caught in her arms long and small,
And therewithal, so sweetly did me kiss,
And softly said: 'Dear heart, how like you this?'

It was no dream: for I lay broad awaking.
But all is turned now through my gentleness,
Into a bitter fashion of forsaking:
And I have leave to go of her goodness,
And she also to use newfangleness.
But, since that I unkindly so am served:
How like you this, what hath she now deserved?

SIR THOMAS WYATT (1503?-1542)

from Mariana

WITH blackest moss the flower-plots
Were thickly crusted, one and all:
The rusted nails fell from the knots
That held the peach to the garden-wall.
The broken sheds looked sad and strange:
Unlifted was the clinking latch;
Weeded and worn the ancient thatch
Upon the lonely moated grange.
She only said, 'My life is dreary,
He cometh not,' she said;
She said, 'I am aweary, aweary,
I would that I were dead!'

Her tears fell with the dews at even;
Her tears fell ere the dews were dried;
She could not look on the sweet heaven,
Either at morn or eventide.
After the flitting of the bats,
When thickest dark did trance the sky,
She drew her casement-curtain by,
And glanced athwart the glooming flats.
She only said, 'The night is dreary,
He cometh not,' she said;
She said, 'I am aweary, aweary,
I would that I were dead!' …

The sparrow's chirrup on the roof,
The slow clock ticking, and the sound
Which to the wooing wind aloof
The poplar made, did all confound
Her sense; but most she loathed the hour
When the thick-moted sunbeam lay
Athwart the chambers, and the day
Was sloping toward his western bower.
Then, said she, 'I am very dreary,
He will not come,' she said;
She wept, 'I am aweary, aweary,
Oh God, that I were dead!'

ALFRED LORD TENNYSON (1809-1892)

The Mower to the Glow-Worms

YE LIVING lamps, by whose dear light
The nightingale does sit so late,
And studying all the summer night,
Her matchless songs does meditate;

Ye country comets, that portend
No war nor prince's funeral,
Shining unto no higher end
Than to presage the grasses fall;

Ye glow-worms, whose officious flame
To wandering mowers shows the way,
That in the night have lost their aim,
And after foolish fires do stray;

Your courteous lights in vain you waste,
Since Juliana here is come,
For she my mind hath so displaced
That I shall never find my home.

ANDREW MARVELL (1621-1678)

To-Night

HARRY, you know at night
The larks in Castle Alley
Sing from the attic's height
As if the electric light
Were the true sun above a summer valley:
Whistle, don't knock, tonight.

I shall come early, Kate;
And we in Castle Alley
Will sit close out of sight
Alone, and ask no light
Of lamp or sun above a summer valley:
Tonight I can stay late.

EDWARD THOMAS (1878-1917)

Time of Roses

IT WAS not in the Winter
Our loving lot was cast;
It was the time of roses—
We plucked them as we passed!

That churlish season never frowned
On early lovers yet:
O no—the world was newly crowned
With flowers when first we met!

'Twas twilight, and I bade you go,
But still you held me fast;
It was the time of roses—
We plucked them as we passed!

THOMAS HOOD (1799-1845)

Anthony's Love for Cleopatra

HOW I loved
Witness, ye days and nights, and all ye hours,
That danced away with down upon your feet,
As all your business were to count my passion!
One day passed by, and nothing saw but love;
Another came, and still 'twas only love:
The suns were wearied out with looking on,
And I untired with loving.
I saw you every day, and all the day;
And every day was still but as the first,
So eager was I still to see you more …

JOHN DRYDEN (1631-1700)
from All for Love

She Walks in Beauty

SHE walks in beauty, like the night
Of cloudless climes and starry skies;
And all that's best of dark and bright
Meet in her aspect and her eyes:
Thus mellowed to that tender light
Which heaven to gaudy day denies.

One shade the more, one ray the less,
Had half impaired the nameless grace
Which waves in every raven tress,
Or softly lightens o'er her face;
Where thoughts serenely sweet express
How pure, how dear their dwelling-place.

And on that cheek, and o'er that brow,
So soft, so calm, yet eloquent,
The smiles that win, the tints that glow,
But tell of days in goodness spent,
A mind at peace with all below,
A heart whose love is innocent!

LORD BYRON (1788-1824)

Bright Star

BRIGHT Star! would I were steadfast as thou art—
Not in lone splendour hung aloft the night,
And watching, with eternal lids apart,
Like Nature's patient sleepless eremite,
The moving waters at their priestlike task
Of pure ablution round earth's human shores,
Or gazing on the new soft-fallen mask
Of snow upon the mountains and the moors—
No—yet still steadfast, still unchangeable,
Pillowed upon my fair love's ripening breast
To feel forever its soft fall and swell,
Awake for ever in a sweet unrest;
Still, still to hear her tender-taken breath,
And so live ever—or else swoon to death.

JOHN KEATS (1795-1821)

Love is Enough

LOVE is enough: though the World be a-waning,
And the woods have no voice but the voice of complaining,
Though the sky be too dark for dim eyes to discover
The gold-cups and daisies fair blooming thereunder,
Though the hills be held shadows, and the sea a dark wonder
And this day draw a veil over all deeds passed over,
Yet their hands shall not tremble, their feet shall not falter;
The void shall not weary, the fear shall not alter
These lips and these eyes of the loved and the lover.

WILLIAM MORRIS (1834-1896)

The Reconcilement

COME, let us now resolve at last
To live and love in quiet;
We'll tie the knot so very fast
That Time shall ne'er untie it.

The truest joys they seldom prove
Who free from quarrels live:
'Tis the most tender part of love
Each other to forgive.

When least I seemed concerned, I took
No pleasure nor no rest;
And when I feigned an angry look,
Alas! I loved you best.

Own but the same to me—you'll find
How blest will be our fate.
O to be happy—to be kind—
Sure never is too late!

JOHN SHEFFIELD,
DUKE OF BUCKINGHAM (1648-1721)

To Chloe

CHLOE, why wish that your years
Would backwards run, till they meet mine,
That perfect likeness, which endears
Things unto things, might us combine?
Our ages so in date agree,
That twins do differ more than we.

There are two births, the one when light
First strikes the new-awakened sense;
The other when two souls unite;
And we must count our life from thence:
When you loved me, and I loved you,
Then both of us were born anew …

And now since you and I are such,
Tell me what's yours, and what is mine?
Our eyes, our ears, our taste, smell, touch,
Do (like our souls) in one combine;
So by this, I as well may be
Too old for you, as you for me.

WILLIAM CARTWRIGHT (1611-1643)

Love's Vision

THERE is no happy life
But in a wife;
The comforts are so sweet
When they do meet:
'Tis plenty, peace, a calm
Like dropping balm:
Love's weather is so fair,
Perfumed air,
Each word such pleasure brings
Like soft-touched strings;
Love's passion moves the heart
On either part.
Such harmony together,
So pleased in either,
No discords, concords still,
Sealed with one will.
By love, God man made one,
Yet not alone;
Like stamps of king and queen
It may be seen,
Two figures but one coin;
So they do join,
Only they not embrace,
We face to face.

WILLIAM CAVENDISH,
DUKE OF NEWCASTLE (1593-1676)

To His Wife on the Fourteenth Anniversary of Her Wedding-Day, with a Ring

'THEE, Mary, with this ring I wed,'
So, fourteen years ago I said.
Behold another ring! 'For what?'
'To wed thee o'er again—why not?'
With that first ring I married youth,
Grace, beauty, innocence, and truth;
Taste long admired, sense long revered,
And all my Molly then appeared.
If she, by merit since disclosed,
Prove twice the woman I supposed,
I plead that double merit now,
To justify a double vow.
Here then, to-day,—with faith as sure,
With ardour as intense and pure,
As when amidst the rites divine
I took thy troth, and plighted mine—
To thee, sweet girl, my second ring,
A token, and a pledge, I bring;
With this I wed, till death us part,
Thy riper virtues to my heart;
Those virtues which, before untried,
The wife has added to the bride—
Those virtues, whose progressive claim,
Endearing wedlock's very name,

My soul enjoys, my song approves,
For conscience' sake as well as love's.
For why?—They show me every hour
honour's high thought, affection's power,
Discretion's deed, sound judgement's sentence,
And teach me all things—but repentance.

SAMUEL BISHOP (1732-1795)

My Old Dutch

I'VE got a pal,
A reg'lar out an' outer,
She's a dear good old gal.
I'll tell yer all about 'er.
It's many years since fust we met,
'Er 'air was then as black as jet;
It's whiter now, but she don't fret,
Not my old gal!

We've been together now for forty years,
An' it don't seem a day too much.
There ain't a lady livin' in the land
As I'd swop for my dear old Dutch.

Sweet fine old gal,
For worlds I wouldn't lose 'er;
She's a dear good old gal,
An' that's what made me choose 'er.
She's stuck to me through thick and thin,
When luck was out, when luck was in.
Ah! wot a wife to me she's been,
An' wot a pal!

ALBERT CHEVALIER (1861-1923)

He is Not Here

DARK house, by which once more I stand
Here in the long unlovely street,
Doors, where my heart was used to beat
So quickly, waiting for a hand,

A hand that can be clasped no more—
Behold me, for I cannot sleep,
And like a guilty thing I creep
At earliest morning to the door.

He is not here; but far away
The noise of life begins again,
And ghastly through the drizzling rain
On the bald street breaks the blank day.

ALFRED, LORD TENNYSON (1809-1892)
from In Memoriam

In Dublin's Fair City

IN DUBLIN'S fair city, where the girls are so pretty,
I first set my eyes on sweet Molly Malone,
As she wheeled her wheel-barrow
Through streets broad and narrow,
Crying, 'Cockles and mussels! alive, alive O!'

Alive, alive O! alive, alive O!
Crying, 'Cockles and mussels! alive, alive O!'

She was a fishmonger, but sure 'twas no wonder,
For so were her father and mother before;
They wheeled a wheel-barrow
Through streets broad and narrow,
Crying, 'Cockles and mussels! alive, alive O!'

She died of a fever, and no one could save her,
And that was the end of sweet Molly Malone;
Now her ghost wheels her barrow
Through streets broad and narrow,
Crying, 'Cockles and mussels! alive, alive O!'

ANON

Barbara Allen

In Scarlet town, where I was born,
There was a fair maid dwellin',
Made every youth cry Well-a-day!
Her name was Barbara Allen.

All in the merry month of May,
When green buds they were swellin',
Young Jemmy Grove on his death-bed lay,
For love of Barbara Allen.

He sent his man in to her then,
To the town where she was dwellin',
'O haste and come to my master dear,
If your name be Barbara Allen.'

So slowly, slowly rose she up,
And slowly she came nigh him,
And when she drew the curtain by—
'Young man, I think you're dyin'.'

'O it's I am sick and very very sick,
And it's all for Barbara Allen.'—
'O the better for me ye'se never be,
Though your heart's blood were a-spillin'!'

'O dinna ye mind, young man,' said she,
'When the red wine ye were fillin',
That ye made the healths go round and round,

III

And slighted Barbara Allen?'
He turned his face unto the wall,
And death was with him dealin':
'Adieu, adieu, my dear friends all,
And be kind to Barbara Allen!'

And slowly, slowly raise she up,
And slowly, slowly left him,
And sighing said she could not stay,
Since death of life had reft him.

As she was walking o'er the fields,
She heard the dead-bell knellin',
And every jow that the dead-bell gave,
Cried 'Woe to Barbara Allen!'

'O mother, mother, make my bed,
O make it saft and narrow:
My love has died for me to-day,
I'll die for him to-morrow.'

'Farewell', she said, 'ye virgins all,
And shun the fault I fell in:
Henceforward take warning by the fall
Of cruel Barbara Allen.'

ANON

Beeny Cliff

O THE opal and the sapphire of that wandering western sea,
And the woman riding high above with bright hair flapping free—
The woman whom I loved so, and who loyally loved me.

The pale mews plained below us, and the waves seemed far away
In a nether sky, engrossed in saying their ceaseless babbling say,
As we laughed light-heartedly aloft on that clear-sunned March day.

A little cloud then cloaked us, and there flew an irised rain,
And the Atlantic dyed its levels with a dull misfeatured stain,
And then the sun burst out again, and purples prinked the main.

—Still in all its chasmal beauty bulks old Beeny to the sky,
And shall she and I not go there once again now March is nigh,
And the sweet things said in that March say anew there by and by?

What if still in chasmal beauty looms that wild weird western shore,
The woman now is—elsewhere—whom the ambling pony bore,
And nor knows nor cares for Beeny, and will laugh there nevermore.

THOMAS HARDY (1840-1928)

from Midnight Lamentation

WHEN you and I go down
Breathless and cold,
Our faces both worn back
To earthly mould,
How lonely we shall be!
What shall we do,
You without me,
I without you?

I cannot bear the thought
You, first, may die,
Nor of how you will weep,
Should I.
We are too much alone;
What can we do
To make our bodies one:
You, me; I, you?

We are most nearly born
Of one same kind;
We have the same delight,
The same true mind.
Must we then part, we part;
Is there no way
To keep a beating heart,
And light of day?

I could now rise and run
Through street on street
To where you are breathing—you,
That we might meet,
And that your living voice
Might sound above
Fear, and we two rejoice
Within our love …

Is, then, nothing safe?
Can we not find
Some everlasting life
In our one mind?
I feel it like disgrace
Only to understand
Your spirit through your word,
Or by your hand.

I cannot find a way
Through love and through;
I cannot reach beyond
Body, to you.
When you or I must go
Down evermore,
There'll be no more to say
—But a locked door.

HAROLD MONRO (1879-1932)

Song

WHEN I am dead, my dearest,
Sing no sad songs for me;
Plant thou no roses at my head,
Nor shady cypress tree:
Be the green grass above me
With showers and dewdrops wet;
And if thou wilt, remember,
And if thou wilt, forget.

I shall not see the shadows,
I shall not feel the rain;
I shall not hear the nightingale
Sing on, as if in pain;
And dreaming through the twilight
That doth not rise nor set,
Haply I may remember,
And haply may forget.

CHRISTINA ROSSETTI (1830-1894)

Helen of Kirkconnell

I wish I were where Helen lies,
Night and day on me she cries:
O that I were where Helen lies,
On fair Kirkconnell lea!

Curst be the heart that thought the thought,
And curst the hand that fired the shot,
When in my arms burd Helen dropped,
And died to succour me!

O, think na ye my heart was sair,
When my Love dropped down and spak nae mair!
I laid her down wi' meikle care
On fair Kirkconnell lea.

As I went down the water side,
None but my foe to be my guide,
None but my foe to be my guide,
On fair Kirkconnell lea:

I lighted down, my sword did draw,
I hacked him in pieces sma',
I hacked him in pieces sma',
For her sake that died for me …

I wish I were where Helen lies;
Night and day on me she cries;
And I am weary of the skies,
For her sake that died for me.

ANON

I Will Give My Love an Apple

I WILL give my love an apple without e'er a core,
I will give my love a house without e'er a door,
I will give my love a palace wherein she may be,
And she may unlock it without e'er a key.

My head is the apple without e'er a core,
My mind is the house without e'er a door,
My heart is the palace wherein she may be,
And she may unlock it without e'er a key.

ANON

How Do I Love Thee?

HOW do I love thee? Let me count the ways.
I love thee to the depth and breadth and height
My soul can reach, when feeling out of sight
For the ends of Being and ideal Grace.
I love thee to the level of every day's
Most quiet need, by sun and candle-light.
I love thee freely, as men strive for right;
I love thee purely, as they turn from praise.
I love thee with the passion put to use
In my old griefs, and with my childhood's faith.
I love thee with a love I seemed to lose
With my lost saints—I love thee with the breath,
Smiles, tears, of all my life!—and, if God choose,
I shall but love thee better after death.

ELIZABETH BARRETT BROWNING (1806-1861)